Philadelphia

★ GREAT ★ CITIES ★ OF THE ★ USA ★

☆ ☆ ☆

LIBRARY OF CONGRESS CATALOGING-IN-PUBLICATION DATA

Loewen, Nancy, 1964-
    Philadelphia / by Nancy Loewen.
       p. cm. -- (Great Cities of the United States)
       Includes index.
    Summary: Introduces the history, economy, and notable attractions of the fifth largest city in the nation.
    ISBN 0-86592-542-9
    1. Philadelphia (Pa.)--Description--1981- --Guide-books--Juvenile literature.
[1. Philadelphia (Pa.)--Description--Guides.] I. Title. II. Series.
F158.18.L57 1989
917.48'110443--dc20

                89-34194
                CIP
                AC

© **1989 Rourke Enterprises, Inc.**

☆ ☆ ☆

Philadelphia

★ GREAT ★ CITIES ★ OF THE ★ USA ★

TEXT BY
NANCY LOEWEN

DESIGN & PRODUCTION BY
MARK E. AHLSTROM
(The Bookworks)

**ROURKE
ENTERPRISES,
INC.**
Vero Beach, FL 32964
U.S.A.

A City
of Contrasts...

☆ ☆ ☆

TABLE OF
CONTENTS

CREDITS
Photos:

Peter Gridley/FPG .... cover photo, 4,
.... 7, 19, 27, 36, 41, 43
Philadelphia Convention & Visitors Bureau
.... 21, 32, 34, 38
Philadelphia Academy of Art/FPG 9
Jim Pickerell/FPG 11
Keystone View Co./FPG 14

James M. Mejuto/FPG 15, 35
Clyde H. Smith/FPG 22
Al Michaud/FPG 23, 39
Louis Goldman/FPG 25
K. Ober/FPG 29
Martin Rogers/FPG 31

TYPESETTING AND LAYOUT: THE FINAL WORD
PRINTING: WORZALLA PUBLISHING CO.

☆ ☆ ☆

A City of Contrasts

Philadelphia is a city of contrasts. In the heart of the downtown area, the statue of a colonial Quaker rises from a stately granite-and-marble building. Nearby, a complex of office buildings asserts a modern presence. Row houses dating back to the 1700's mix with sleek high-rise apartments and condominiums. Tree-lined public squares preserve the feeling of a friendly country town.

Perhaps more than any other U.S. city, Philadelphia celebrates its past while looking to the future. Certainly its past is impressive. It was here that 13 American colonies declared their independence from England. Here, too, such great leaders as George Washington, James Madison, and Benjamin Franklin created the very foundation of the United States: its Constitution.

Those and other events have given Philadelphia a sense of dignity and purpose that will always remain. Yet there is another side to the city—a louder, more carefree side. Philadelphia is a city known for its vocal sports fans and for its boisterous Italian Market. It's a city that holds an enormous parade just to salute a song—Richard Berry's "Louie Louie." It's a city that, some say, has the best soft pretzels, hoagies, and cheesesteaks in the world.

Philadelphia is located in the southeastern corner of Pennsylvania, along the Delaware River. Besides being the state's largest city, Philadelphia is also the fifth largest city in the nation. The population is about three-fifths white, and most of the rest are black. In 1985, famous map-makers Rand McNally ranked Philadelphia fifth among the 50 best places to live in the United States. Philadelphians weren't surprised. They'd known it all along.

The downtown area of Philadelphia was planned by William Penn in 1682. The buildings all came later!

William Penn's "Holy Experiment"

During the 1600's, European nations were eager to establish colonies in the "new world" of North America. The area of today's Pennsylvania came under British control in 1675.

At that time, a man named William Penn was living in England. He was a member of the Society of Friends, commonly called Quakers. This was a religious group that believed in a simple style of worship. Quakers also believed in equal rights for women, and were against war and slavery. At that time, their views were thought to be very radical.

The Quakers—and other religious groups—were often persecuted because they spoke out against the Anglican Church of England. People were afraid that the nation would collapse if people were allowed to hold different religious views.

William Penn didn't agree. He thought people of different faiths **could** live together peacefully, and set out to prove it.

Penn's late father was owed a great deal of money by the English government. As his father's heir, Penn approached King Charles II with a bold plan. Why not pay him back with land in the New World? There he would set up his "holy experiment."

King Charles II agreed with the plan right away. He was tired of Penn criticizing the English establishment. Besides, it was a cheap way for King Charles to settle his debt! On March 14, 1681, Penn was granted a charter for much of what is today's Pennsylvania.

William Penn planned his experiment very carefully. Besides promising religious tolerance, he guaranteed every taxpayer a vote, all trials by jury, and taxation only by law. His critics were scornful of his plans. "This will never work!" they laughed. "They'll be fighting in no time."

In 1682, William Penn and about 100 Quaker colonists sailed up the Delaware River to found the city of Philadelphia. This city—whose name means "Brotherly Love"— would be the capital of the Pennsylvania Colony.

Settlers from Sweden, Holland, Ireland, Finland, and other countries were already living in the area. They were soon joined by more European settlers, fleeing such problems as famine and persecution. Other settlers were more interested in the economic opportunities the new state was likely to provide.

William Penn's "holy experiment" worked. People of different

William Penn got along well with the Native Americans. This painting depicts a treaty he signed with the Delaware tribe.

nationalities and faiths lived and worked side by side. What's more, there was no fighting with the Delaware Indians, who also lived in that area. Penn's appeal for a "just and friendly conduct toward the natives" was followed. Philadelphia was the only town built in that period that did not need to fortify itself against the Indians.

Thanks to fertile land and a good harbor on the Delaware River, Philadelphia grew quickly. It was incorporated as a city in 1701, with a population of about 4,500. And by 1720, the population numbered 10,000.

The Influence of Ben Franklin

Benjamin Franklin was another important person in Philadelphia's past. He was just a poor 17-year-old when he moved to Philadelphia from Boston in 1723. Within a few years, however, he had become Philadelphia's best-known civic leader. Though some people grumbled about him and called him an eccentric, he contributed a great deal to both Philadelphia and the nation.

During his lifetime, Ben Franklin took on many roles: diplomat, philosopher, scientist, and more. His work in publishing and printing turned Philadelphia into the publishing center of the Colonies. When he took over the *Pennsylvania Gazette*, a newspaper, he increased circulation and introduced new techniques in the printing process. Today, however, he is best known for the *Poor Richard's Almanac*. This collection of witty proverbs was published from 1733 to 1758. Many of his sayings are in common use today, such as "a penny saved is a penny earned."

Practical and civic-minded, Ben Franklin left behind a long list of "firsts." He founded Pennsylvania Hospital, the nation's first hospital. He established the first public library, called the Library Company of Philadelphia. He also founded the American Philosophical Society, an important scientific organization, and the Academy of Philadelphia. The

The Ben Franklin Bridge connects Philadelphia with New Jersey.

Academy later became the University of Pennsylvania, one of the nation's oldest universities.

Yet it was Ben Franklin's scientific accomplishments that made his name a household word during this period. The invention of bifocals, the Franklin stove, and the lightning rod improved the lives of many colonists.

Throughout Philadelphia, many buildings, parks, and other structures carry his name. At the foot of the Ben Franklin Bridge is a huge sculpture of a lightning bolt. The 30-ton, 96-foot sculpture, created by sculptor Isamu Noguchi, honors Ben Franklin's most famous scientific experiment—flying a kite in a thunderstorm.

We Hold These Truths ...

By the mid-1700's Philadelphia was the leading city in the Colonies. It was centrally located besides, and became a natural headquarters for the Colonies during the American Revolution.

For some time, the Colonies had resented the unfair trade and tax policies England had been trying to force on them. In September 1774, delegates from 12 of the 13 Colonies were sent to Carpenters' Hall in Philadelphia to discuss the situation. This is known as the First Continental Congress. The 56 delegates denied England the right to tax the Colonies, and agreed not to conduct business with English traders.

England, who had already sent soldiers to oversee the Colonies, would not accept their position. The two sides clashed in the battles of Lexington and Concord, near Boston, in April 1775.

The next month, the Second Continental Congress quickly convened in Philadelphia. This time Congress met in Philadelphia's State House, later called Independence Hall. On June 16, 1775, Congress named the tall and dignified George Washington as commander-in-chief of the Continental Army. The bloody Battle of Bunker Hill soon followed.

Also in June, Congress appointed a committee to prepare a document proclaiming the Colonies' independence from England. A 33-year-old Virginian named Thomas Jefferson worked on the first draft. After receiving the approval of the committee, the document was sent to Congress for debate and revision. And on July 4, 1776, the Declaration of Independence was approved by Congress in Philadelphia.

British Occupation

Although so many historic decisions were being made in their city, not all Philadelphians supported the Revolutionary War at first. There were several reasons. Merchants were worried about losing their businesses. Some members of the upper class were still loyal to the Crown. And many of the Quakers refused to bear arms because it went against their religious beliefs.

Philadelphia was touched directly by the war in early fall of 1777. On September 25, after the Battle of Brandywine Creek, the city was overtaken by British General William Howe and 18,000 British soldiers. Soon afterwards, the Americans were defeated again in the Battle of Germantown.

Members of the Continental Congress fled from the city. Thousands of citizens did the same, abandoning their homes to the British troops. British soldiers spent a comfortable winter in the city. In the meantime, General Washington and the American troops suffered a hard winter in nearby Valley Forge.

That spring, France joined the American side in the war. The British troops withdrew from Philadelphia on June 18, 1778, when they heard that a fleet of French ships was on its way to the city. The Continental Congress soon came back to Philadelphia.

Fighting came to an end with England's surrender in October 1781. However, the Revolutionary War wasn't formally over until 1783, when both sides signed a treaty in Paris.

Birth of a Nation

Though the Americans had won the war, their political problems were hardly over. The Articles of Confederation, adopted in 1781, made the central government very dependent on the states for money and executive powers. This loose structure created a nation that wasn't very strong. The United States wasn't well regarded in Europe. It was in debt. And interstate trading regulations—which varied greatly—were creating serious conflicts between some states.

To work out these problems, the states sent delegates to the Constitutional Convention in Philadelphia. Traveling by stagecoach and by boat, the delegates came to the city during the hot spring and summer of 1787. Among them were George Wash-

This drawing shows Ben Franklin (left) in a discussion with the leaders who drafted the Declaration of Independence.

ington, James Madison, and Alexander Hamilton.

Meeting in Philadelphia's Independence Hall, the delegates spent long hours trying to come up with a workable plan to govern the new nation. The result of their many discussions and debates was the United States Constitution. It provided for a government of three separate branches: executive, judicial, and legislative. In addition, the Bill of Rights guaranteed basic individual freedoms.

On September 17, 1787, the delegates signed the document that has survived into the 20th century with few changes. The Constitution was then sent to the state governments for ratification.

Philadelphia was the official capital of the United States from

1790 to 1800, except for a brief time when New York City held that post. George Washington, the first President of the United States, served most of his presidency in Philadelphia. John Adams, his successor, served three years in the city. The capital was moved to Washington, D.C., in 1800. At one point, plans were made to move the capital back to Philadelphia, but this never happened.

During this time, Philadelphia also lost its position as the capital of Pennsylvania, which was moved to Lancaster. Today, Pennsylvania's capital is the city of Harrisburg.

Changes Ahead

The 1790's were a very difficult period for Philadelphians. An epidemic of yellow fever spread throughout the city. About 5,000 people, or one out of every 10 citizens, died from the disease.

Still, Philadelphia continued to hold an important place in the nation. It became a center of education and medical research, positions the city still holds today. Law, finance, and publishing also flourished here. In less than thirty years, Philadelphia's population nearly tripled.

Delegates to the Constitutional Convention in 1787 often met at the City Tavern to discuss important issues in a relaxed setting. The Tavern has been reconstructed and is a popular tourist attraction.

Although Philadelphia would always be a great city, it began losing ground to New York City around 1820. Bypassing Philadelphia in population, New York also took over as the leading commercial and financial center of the United States.

Philadelphia now turned its attention to manufacturing. Coal mines west of Philadelphia provided fuel for factories and for export. The city began producing items such as textiles, clothing, machinery, locomotives, and ships. The market for such items expanded when a new system of railroads connected the city with the rest of the nation.

As Philadelphia's industries grew, so did the city. A wave of immigration from 1830 to 1880 brought many Irish and German people into the Philadelphia area. During this time, however, machines began replacing people at the factories. Competition for jobs was often intense.

This situation, along with deteriorating housing and increased crime, caused hard feelings between some of the native Philadelphians and the immigrants. In 1844, riots between Protestants and Irish Roman Catholics killed 30 people. William Penn's legacy of brotherhood was, for a time, forgotten.

The relationship between whites and blacks was often no better. The city's small black community was segregated from the whites. Blacks were denied the vote, and were discriminated against in other ways. Six major race riots broke out in the decades before the Civil War.

At the same time, Philadelphia's Quaker population was very active in the anti-slavery movement. A Quaker woman named Lucretia Mott, along with several others, founded the American Anti-Slavery Society. Mott and her husband also organized "free stores" in Philadelphia. These stores sold only those products that were made with free, or non-slave, labor. Lucretia Mott later became an important leader in the women's rights movement.

The Civil War

Although Philadelphia wasn't united on the racial issue, it believed strongly in preserving the Union. Most citizens stood behind the Union when the Civil War began in 1861. An organization called the Union League was formed to raise money for the Union troops. Textile and clothing plants churned out uniforms, blankets, shoes, and boots. Railroad cars were built to transport Union troops and supplies. Ships were made for the Union blockades.

Located just above the Mason-Dixon Line, Philadelphia became known as the "Gateway to the South." Union troops passed through the city on their way to battles in the South. Philadelphia's many hospitals and doctors also cared for thousands of wounded soldiers.

The Civil War came to an end in April 1865. Philadelphia greeted this good news with fireworks and the ringing of all the city's bells. But the festive mood in the city—and the nation—was cut short when President Abraham Lincoln was assassinated.

The train carrying Lincoln's body arrived in Philadelphia on April 22, on its way to Springfield, Illinois.

Until midnight that day, the coffin lay in Philadelphia's Independence Hall. In a funeral procession several miles long, 85,000 Philadelphians passed before the coffin to pay tribute to the great leader.

Apples 5¢

After the Civil War, Philadelphia's population continued to grow. From 1880 to 1925, large numbers of Jews, Italians, Poles, and Slavs came to the city from Europe. Whites and blacks from the rural South journeyed to Philadelphia in search of better jobs. By 1900, nearly 1,294,000 people lived in the city.

When World War I began, the city united once more in a war effort. Philadelphia's young men volunteered for the army. Meanwhile, those at home worked in war-related factories and grew "victory gardens." Shortages of food, coal, and other items were willingly suffered for the cause of the war.

In 1918, war of a different sort hit the city. An epidemic of influenza was spreading through the country.

In Philadelphia, the first death from the illness was on September 18. Two weeks later, more than 4,000 Philadelphians were dead. Schools and churches shut down as people stayed in their homes, fearing that they or their loved ones would come down with the dreaded disease.

The Great Depression of the 1930's also affected Philadelphia. The soup kitchens and shelters that opened were not enough to take care of all the jobless people. Apple-sellers lined Philadelphia's busy intersections, holding signs that read: "Unemployed...Apples 5¢."

Times slowly got better. But many Depression-scarred Philadelphians were unwilling to give their employers as much power as they'd had in the past. More Philadelphians joined unions. Many strikes—sometimes violent—occurred during this time.

Philadelphia Renaissance

During World War II, many Quaker communities were active in providing humanitarian care for victims of war. The American Friends Service Committee, with headquarters in Philadelphia, was awarded the Nobel Peace Prize in 1947. The influence of the Quakers is still felt today, particularly in the nuclear-freeze movement.

In Philadelphia, the period after World War II was marked by a great renovation movement. Local, state, and federal governments joined with private citizens to create what was called the "Philadelphia Renaissance." Old, substandard buildings were replaced with new ones. Thousands of other homes were restored. This movement, still going on today, has made a very noticeable difference in the look of the city.

As "the city that gave birth to a nation," Philadelphia has been in the world spotlight in recent years. The 200th anniversary of the signing of the Declaration of Independence and the Constitution has prompted many grand celebrations.

One of these was a special session of Congress held in Independence Hall. Back in 1787, delegates approved the "great compromise" of

This is the modern face of downtown Philadelphia at sunset.

a bicameral, or two-house, legislature. Two hundred years later, modern senators and representatives met in Independence Hall to take part in anniversary ceremonies.

Time had certainly brought its changes. In 1987, the lawmakers at Independence Hall included women, blacks, and other minorities. Nearby, people demonstrated for such causes as the Equal Rights Amendment and the abolishment of apartheid in South Africa.

That's Philadelphia, after all—rooted in the past, but always looking forward.

INSIDE PHILADELPHIA

Center City

Philadelphia covers an area of 144 square miles. In 1854 the city was merged with Philadelphia County, so the boundaries of the city and the county are the same. The metropolitan area covers an additional 3,600 square miles and has a population of nearly five million.

Downtown Philadelphia—"Center City"—is located between two rivers. The Delaware River flows southwest toward the Atlantic Ocean. It forms the eastern boundary between Pennsylvania and New Jersey. The Schuylkill River flows into the Delaware from the northwest. In this "V" lies Center City.

Center City forms the core of Philadelphia's government, business, and cultural activities. The largest department stores and hotels are located here. Many fine libraries, theaters, and museums are found in Center City as well. Railroad, subway, and bus terminals provide transportation within the city and beyond.

Besides being the heart of modern Philadelphia, Center City is also the heart of historical Philadelphia. The area was planned by William Penn and a surveyor in 1682. Penn, who envisioned Philadelphia as a "green country town," made sure to include five squares, or park areas— one in the center and four in each corner. These squares still exist today.

Penn Square lies in the center of the city and is home of the impressive Philadelphia City Hall. This building, made of granite and marble, was completed in 1901 in the French Renaissance style. It's one of the biggest City Halls in the United States. And that's not all: on top of the building sits a 37-foot bronze

Built of stone, the Philadelphia City Hall is located on Penn Square.

The Philadelphia Library is located along the tree-lined Ben Franklin Parkway.

statue of William Penn. It's the world's largest sculpture on top of a building.

Until recently, the City Hall building was the tallest building in Philadelphia. Even though there was no law banning taller buildings, tradition kept such buildings from being constructed. Then, in 1984, developers proposed putting up two office towers that broke the height barrier.

This spurred a great public debate. Some citizens, wanting to uphold tradition, thought the office towers should not be built. Others thought that Philadelphia needed such buildings to show the world the city's modern side. This school of thought won out, and the office towers were built.

The Ben Franklin Parkway stretches northwest from City Hall to the Philadelphia Museum of Art. Modeled after France's famous

☆ **22** ☆

Rittenhouse Square is a popular meeting place among Philadelphians. There's almost always something to see or do.

"Champs Elysées," the parkway is a broad, tree-lined boulevard with flowers and fountains. It passes through Logan Circle, another one of William Penn's public squares. Several famous museums are located here, along with the Cathedral of St. Peter and Paul. To many Philadelphians, Logan Circle is one of the prettiest sections of the city.

Rittenhouse Square is located about six blocks south of Logan Circle. It was named after the famous astronomer and Philadelphia native, David Rittenhouse. It, too, has tree-lined walkways. Flower shows, art exhibits, or concerts are often held here in the summer. Surrounding it are many condominiums and high-rise apartments.

East of Rittenhouse Square is Washington Square. It was named for George Washington on the 100th anniversary of his birth. Fittingly, the Memorial to Unknown Soldiers of the American Revolution is located here. Franklin Square, named after Ben Franklin, lies to the north.

Between Washington and Franklin Squares and slightly east is the Independence National Historic Park. The park contains many buildings that were important during the American Revolution.

Center City's Neighborhoods

Center City is also where many Philadelphians live. Unlike the central districts of other large cities, however, downtown Philadelphia is not plagued by poverty. People live in modern high-rise apartment buildings, or in row houses and townhouses from the 1800's. Most of these residents are professional people who can afford the high rent.

Society Hill is a neighborhood in Center City that is often praised for its renovation efforts. During colonial times, it was the home of many important political leaders and wealthy people. As the city grew, however, these people moved west. By the end of World War I, Society Hill had become a slum.

A restoration effort in the 1950's turned the slum back into an upscale neighborhood. Society Hill now has hundreds of restored 200-year-old homes. Some of the nation's oldest churches can be found here, too. Many blocks look almost as they did in colonial times—except for the expensive cars on the streets!

Elfreth's Alley is another well-known neighborhood in Center City. Along this narrow cobblestone street are 35 brick homes that were built during early 1700's. People still live in these homes. In fact, Elfreth's Alley is said to be the oldest street of continuously occupied homes in the nation. On Elfreth's Alley Day, held each June, many of the residents open up their homes to the public.

Many of Philadelphia's 80,000 Asians live in Chinatown, west of Franklin Square. Here the street signs are in two languages and the phone booths have pagoda tops. Ethnic restaurants and stores line the main streets.

Beyond Center City

South Philadelphia is the oldest section of Philadelphia. Swedish people first settled in today's neighborhood of Southwark in 1638. By the 1800's, it was home to Irish immigrants and a small community of blacks. Then, between 1880 and 1930, a large number of Eastern European Jews and Italians moved into the area.

Today, Italians are the largest group living in South Philadelphia —often called "Little Italy." It was here that Rocky, played by Sylvester Stallone in the *Rocky* movies, grew up. South Philadelphia's real-life stars include singer Marian Anderson, tenor Mario Lanza, and actor Eddie Fisher.

Little Italy's Open Market is a big hit with the tourists and natives alike. In this five-block-long display of produce and crafts, people can bargain over everything from live chickens to designer handbags.

The homes in Elfreth's Alley were built in the 1700's, and they are still lived in today.

West Philadelphia lies beyond the Schuylkill River. This hilly area began as a residential suburb for the rich. In the 1920's, however, it became a working-class neighborhood. Today, blacks are the main group living here.

Just across the river from Center City is an area of hospitals and schools known as "University City." These include the University of Pennsylvania and its hospital, Drexel University, and the University City Science Center. More than 32,000 students live here. The Civic Center also draws many convention-goers.

North Philadelphia is the most densely populated section of the city. It was formed after the Civil War, when many black people came to the city to live. Philadelphia's renovation efforts after World War II have improved some neighborhoods in northern Philadelphia. Still, large areas are getting more run down each year. Many of Philadelphia's poorest people live here.

There are some strong signs of hope here as well, however. In 1964, Minister Leon H. Sullivan founded the Opportunities Industrialization Center. This center, called OIC, helps train blacks for jobs. In addition, many black cultural institutions are found here, including Progress Plaza, a black-owned shopping center.

The most famous neighborhood in northwestern Philadelphia is Germantown. Settled in 1683 by a group of 13 German Quaker and Mennonite families, it was the first German settlement in America. A group of young, well-off Anglicans and Presbyterians built summer homes there during the 1800's. Many of these have been restored.

Germantown was an important neighborhood around the period of the Civil War. The first written protest of slavery came from its residents. And the Johnson House was a stop in the Underground Railroad, which helped black slaves escape to freedom in the North.

The northeast section of Philadelphia covers the most land. It was settled after World War II, and includes mostly middle-class people from Jewish, Polish, or Italian backgrounds.

Beyond Philadelphia itself is its extensive metropolitan area. It covers four counties in Pennsylvania and another three in New Jersey. Thousands of these residents commute to the city each day by car, bus, or train.

The "Main Line" is perhaps Philadelphia's best-known suburban area. In the mid-1800's, the Pennsylvania Railroad opened a commuter route from the city to the western suburbs. Wealthy people soon moved to a string of towns along the route. Many of Philadelphia's elite still live there, in communities such as Devon and Bryn Mawr.

Like downtown Philadelphia, the metropolitan area has several sites made famous by the American Revolution. These include Valley Forge and the Brandywine Battlefield.

The Schuylkill River separates West Philadelphia from Center City.

GETTING AROUND

Like most cities, Philadelphia's neighborhoods have been affected by advances in transportation. In the Colonial period, rich and poor Philadelphians often lived side by side. The only way to get around—besides walking—was to take horse-drawn stagecoaches. The problem was that stagecoaches were expensive and could carry only a few people at a time.

Then, in the late 1850's, "horse-cars" carried dozens of people along iron rails laid in the streets. This was still too expensive for most people. However, many professional people now found it easier to leave the central area.

The advent of electric trolleys, subways, and automobiles changed the city even more. More than ever, residential districts became divided by income, race, and ethnic origin.

Today, the publicly owned Southeastern Pennsylvania Transportation Authority (SEPTA) provides the city with local transportation. The system includes buses, elevated trains, subways, streetcars, and a few trolleys. Because of the congested downtown area, using public transportation is usually more convenient than driving.

Just seven miles from downtown is the Philadelphia International Airport, which handles 15 airlines. A smaller airport nearby handles private and commuter planes. Penn Central and Reading railroads provide national passenger and freight service. A "commuter tunnel" connects 13 rail commuter lines from the Philadelphia region.

Philadelphia has a wide variety of public transportation. This is one of the few old trolleys that are still being used in the city.

INDUSTRY & TRADE

Philadelphia was once a world manufacturing center. During the 1970's, however, manufacturing declined by about 40 percent. Today, the focus has shifted to service industries such as education, tourism, and health care.

Philadelphia has about 50 hospitals, including the Pennsylvania Hospital and the U.S. Naval Hospital. Its six medical schools include the University of Pennsylvania Medical School and the Thomas Jefferson University Medical School. Philadelphia also has two dental schools and many research institutions.

Philadelphia is second only to Boston in concentration of schools. Within the city are more than 20 colleges and universities. Another 30 are nearby. These schools are attended by more than 150,000 full- and part-time students.

In a city so rich with history, tourism also contributes a great deal to the local economy. Each year, millions of people come to Philadelphia to see the sights. These tourists help support Philadelphia's hotels, restaurants, shops, and local transportation.

Since colonial times, Philadelphia has been considered an important financial center. The Third Federal Reserve District Bank is located here, along with many other large banks and insurance companies. Here, too, the United States Mint—the largest in the world—makes the coins used by Americans every day. The mint produces more than $350 million worth of coins each year. Visitors can actually watch the coins being made.

The "Ports of Philadelphia" complex is one of the busiest freshwater ports in the world. The port

The Philadelphia Stock Exchange is an important part of the financial industry.

serves many industries, including oil refining, shipbuilding, and steelmaking. The major exports are grain and coal.

Although manufacturing has been steadily declining, it remains an important part of Philadelphia's economy. The city ranks third in production of clothing, behind New York and Los Angeles. Other products include pharmaceuticals and other chemicals, metal cans, sheet metal, bakery products, and beverages.

"The Most Historic Square Mile in America"

Independence National Historic Park is the most famous Philadelphia attraction—and with good reason. The park covers 40 acres and includes about 40 historical buildings.

Both the Declaration of Independence and the United States Constitution were signed at Independence Hall. This brick building, built in 1732, still holds an air of

Next to the Liberty Bell, Independence Hall is probably Philadelphia's most popular attraction.

solemn accomplishment. Tourists can see the silver inkstand the delegates used when signing the Declaration of Independence. Here, too, is the "Rising Sun" chair from which George Washington took part in the Constitutional Convention.

Visitors can also see Congress Hall, where the United States Congress met from 1790 to 1800. In this building, George Washington was inaugurated for his second term. John Adams, the second President of the United States, was also inaugurated here.

Liberty Bell Pavilion holds the world's most famous bell. It is commonly believed that the Liberty Bell was rung in 1776 to announce to Philadelphians the first reading of the Declaration of Independence. From 1753 to 1976, the Liberty Bell hung in the belfry of Independence Hall. Then it was moved to its present site, where it is surrounded by glass.

The Liberty Bell has an ironic story behind it. It was originally ordered from England to mark the 50th anniversary of Philadelphia's city charter. But the clapper cracked the bell the very first time it was rung! Two skilled Philadelphia foundrymen managed to recast it, and the bell was used for many years.

In 1835, the bell cracked yet again while ringing for the funeral of Chief Justice John Marshall. That time the bell would remain cracked.

Other attractions in Independence National Historic Park are Carpenters' Hall, the meeting place of the first Continental Congress; the Army/Navy Museum; and the Second Bank of the United States.

Other Historical Sites

Although not officially part of Independence Park, there are many other popular tourist spots nearby. One of them is the Betsy Ross House. Legend has it that a woman named Betsy Ross stitched the first United States flag in 1776. Although this hasn't been proven, people like to visit the house anyway. The restored home shows how the middle class lived during this period.

The Liberty Bell is located in the Liberty Bell Pavilion, where it is surrounded by glass.

Writer Edgar Allan Poe lived in Philadelphia for six years during the 1840's. During this time, he published some of his best-known stories. One of them, "The Gold Bug," is considered the first modern detective story. Today, at the Edgar Allan Poe National Historic Site, people can see the home in which these stories were created.

On a grander scale is Penn's Landing, which marks the area of William Penn's first entry into the New World. Penn's Landing covers 37 acres and includes a museum, a collection of historic ships, and a sculpture garden. Recently, an expensive complex of shops, cafés, movie theaters, and restaurants was added to the area.

Fairmount Park stretches along both sides of the Schuylkill River.

Penn's Landing includes a collection of old ships, as well as other interesting things to see. The William Penn Bridge is in the background.

This beautiful wooded area is lined with walkways, bicycle trails, and jogging paths. It sprawls over 8,500 acres, and is the largest landscaped city-owned park in the world. The park includes concert halls, a zoo, and a Japanese teahouse.

The Centennial Exposition was held in Fairmount Park in 1876. This celebration marked the 100th anniversary of the Declaration of Independence. It was considered the grandest fair of its time. Foreign nations sent their best machinery, art, and other items to be displayed at the fair. Between May and November of 1876, nearly 10 million people passed through the gates. More than one hundred buildings were erected for the fair. Of those, only two remain today.

The Philadelphia Museum of Art is a very impressive building!

Museums

Philadelphia is well known for its many interesting museums. Four of the city's most noted ones are found in or near Fairmount Park. The Philadelphia Museum of Art rises up majestically at the end of the Ben Franklin Parkway. One of the world's most noted art museums, it has more than 500,000 objects on display. These range from ancient Chinese clay figures to contemporary American prints and photographs. The works of many French masters are shown there as well, including those of Rubens, Renoir, Monet, and Van Gogh.

The works of French sculptor Auguste Rodin are displayed nearby in the Rodin Museum. More than 200 works—including "The Thinker" and "The Gates of Hell'—can be seen there. Rodin, who died in 1917, is thought to be the best sculptor since Michelangelo.

The Franklin Science Institute was the first museum to display science and technology exhibits. Its do-it-yourself exhibits cover topics such as communication, nuclear energy, and even space travel. Here people can learn about the human heart—by actually walking through a giant model!

Founded in 1812, the Academy of Natural Sciences is the oldest museum of its kind in the nation. Its displays include animals, birds, insects, and minerals. The most breathtaking display, however, is the skeleton of a 65-million-year-old dinosaur—over two stories tall.

Sports

Philadelphia's professional sports teams are well-supported by the city.

People here buy more tickets to pro games than do residents of any other U.S. city!

Playing in Vet's Stadium in South Philadelphia are baseball's Phillies and football's Eagles. In the Spectrum, also in South Philadelphia, the Philadelphia Flyers hockey team tries for goals. Here, too, the 76ers play basketball for the NBA.

Philadelphia native Wilt "the Stilt" Chamberlain started his career playing for the 76ers. Another local success story is that of Joe Frazier, who defeated Muhammed Ali in 1971 to become the heavyweight champion of the world. Then there's baseball's legendary manager, Connie Mack. From 1901 to 1950, Mack led the Philadelphia Athletics to nine pennants and five championships.

Philadelphia is home of the "Big Five" in college basketball, which includes La Salle University and the University of Pennsylvania. And each year the classic Army-Navy football game is played in Philadelphia the weekend after Thanksgiving.

Philadelphia's "Boat House Row" has a unique beauty.

The Schuylkill River is the setting for many boat races. Along Kelly Drive is "Boat House Row," where the shoreline houses are strung up with little white lights. In the springtime, the best college rowing and sculling crews compete for national titles. Incidentally, Kelly Drive is named for yet another famous Philadelphia native—the late Grace Kelly, an actress who through marriage became the Princess of Monaco.

The Arts

An extravagant ball marked the opening of the Academy of Music in 1857. Today, going to an Academy performance is still a special event. As the oldest U.S. opera house still in use, the Academy houses the Philadelphia Ballet and the Philly Pops, in addition to the Opera Company of Philadelphia.

The Academy's biggest attraction, however, is the Philadelphia Orchestra. Philadelphians are proud of their world-renowned orchestra, whose famous conductors have included Eugene Ormandy and Leopold Stokowski. The Philadelphia Orchestra plays in the Academy from September to May. During the summer, the orchestra performs in Fairmount Park.

Philadelphia has made its contribution to pop music as well. Dick Clark's "American Bandstand" began here as a local dance show. When the show went national in 1957, it took the careers of Fabian, Frankie Avalon, and Chubby Checker right along with it.

The visual arts have also gotten strong support in Philadelphia. A law passed in 1958 required that one percent of the cost of all new buildings—both public and private—had to be used to buy art for the city. This has resulted in the purchase of many fine works enjoyed by native Philadelphians and tourists alike.

The Academy of Music is the oldest opera house still being used in the United States.

GOVERNING THE PEOPLE

In 1951, Philadelphia voters approved a "strong mayor" system. This gave more power to the mayor and executive branch. Before then, the city government needed approval from the Pennsylvania General Assembly to levy taxes and act on other local matters.

The mayor is elected for a four-year term. A mayor can serve an unlimited number of terms—but no more than two in a row. The mayor appoints a four-member cabinet consisting of the city solicitor, finance director, city representative/director of commerce, and city manager.

The city council is the lawmaking branch of the city government. Philadelphia's 17-member city council is elected for four-year terms. Ten council members are elected by voters in 10 districts, while seven are elected by the city as a whole.

Under the strong mayor system, the mayor has the power to appoint officials, veto laws, and prepare the city budget. However, the council can override the mayor with a two-thirds majority vote.

The Philadelphia city government receives its money by taxing wages. Because this is not enough money to run the city, the state and federal governments also contribute.

From the time of the Civil War to the early 1950's, Philadelphia was controlled by a group of Republican officials often accused of corruption. But if the Philadelphians knew about the corruption, they didn't seem to care—until 1951, that is. At that time, Joseph S. Clark, a Democratic reformer, was elected mayor. Democrats have been elected since then. In 1983, W. Wilson Goode became Philadelphia's first black mayor. He was re-elected in 1987.

Until 1984, City Hall was the tallest building in Philadelphia. It is located on the southeast end of Ben Franklin Parkway.

FINDING A BETTER WAY

Philadelphia, like all large cities, faces many challenges. Poverty and unemployment are the most pressing problems. After World War II, many poor people came to the city. At the same time, middle-class people began moving to the wealthier suburbs. Because Philadelphia's city budget depends on taxed wages, this means that the city is receiving less money in a time when more money is urgently needed. Limited state and federal funds add to the problem.

Today's shifting economy is partly responsible for this situation. With manufacturing in a decline, many factories are standing vacant. Affected most are the people without the education or job skills required for most service-industry jobs. Some of these people move away from Philadelphia. Others take on low-paying jobs, and struggle to make ends meet. Many end up on welfare.

With poverty and unemployment comes high crime. Philadelphia has been battling a high crime rate for many years. In fact, the police department has been the largest single expense in the city budget. So far, however, this has yet to bring about any lasting change.

Unsafe or decaying housing is another serious problem in Philadelphia. By one estimate, there are up to 30,000 homes that have been abandoned by owners who couldn't afford to repair them. The same number probably ought to be abandoned.

With this problem, however, Philadelphia is having better success. A program now offers certain buildings at bargain rates to people who pledge to repair the houses and live in them. Many young professionals are jumping at this chance.

Neighborhoods are slowly but surely being improved.

The restoration drive has also affected public property. Independence National Park, for instance, was not always the neatly organized park it is today. At one time, factories and warehouses crowded the area. Together with the National Park Service, Philadelphia began cleaning up the area in 1951—tearing down some buildings and restoring others. The success has been encouraging, and has boosted tourism in the city.

Philadelphia's approach to renovation is more focused than that of other large cities, and it shows. "We want a city not only **of** but also **for** people—just as Penn did," city planner Edmund Bacon once said to *National Geographic*. "In fact, we're getting back to his original concept, and it's working fine."

Heading into the 21st century, Philadelphia is still making things happen.

Philadelphia has been working hard to restore itself—and it shows!

*Philadelphia, Pennsylvania

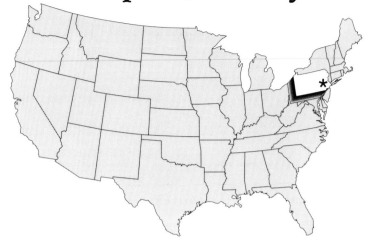

IMPORTANT FACTS

- Population: 1,642,900 (1986 estimate)
  Rank: 5
- Population of metropolitan area: 4,825,700
- Mayor: W. Wilson Goode (next election, November 1991)
- Seat of Philadelphia County

- Land area: 136 sq. miles
- Monthly normal temperature:
  January—31.2°F
  July—76.5°F
- Average annual precipitation: 41.42"
- Latitude: 39° 56' 58" N
- Longitude: 75° 09' 21" W
- Altitude: ranges from sea level to 440 ft.

- Time zone: Eastern

- Annual events:
  Mummers Parade, January 1
  Philadelphia Open House, May
  Elfreth's Alley Fête Day, June
  Freedom Festival, July
  Thanksgiving Day Parade, November
  Army-Navy Football Game, November
  Historical Christmas Tours, Fairmount
    Park, December

IMPORTANT DATES

1675—Pennsylvania area under British rule.
1681—William Penn granted charter for Pennsylvania.
1682—Philadelphia founded.
1701—Philadelphia incorporated as city.
1774—First Continental Congress met at Carpenters' Hall.
1775—American Revolution began.
1776—Declaration of Independence approved.
1777—Philadelphia occupied by British troops.
1781—Articles of Confederation adopted.
1787—delegates to Consititional Convention approved United States Constitution.
1790-1800—Philadelphia served as nation's capital.
1854—city of Philadelphia merged with Phildelphia County.
1876—Centennial Exposition held in Fairmount Park.
1947—American Friends Service Committee (Quakers) won Nobel Peace Prize.
1951—"strong mayor" system approved.
1985—Philadelphia ranked fifth among 50 best places to live.
1987—Philadelphia celebrated 200th anniversary of U.S. Constitution.

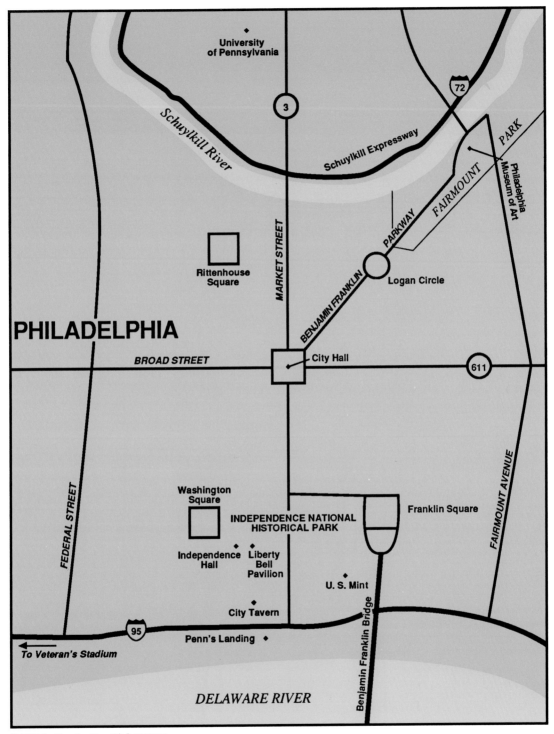

PHILADELPHIA

©1989 Mark E. Ahlstrom

GLOSSARY

astronomer—a scientist who studies the stars and planets.

bicameral—having two legislative chambers. The United States Congress consists of the House of Representatives and the Senate.

charter—a written document that defines rights and obligations of a group.

cheesesteak—fried beef and Cheddar cheese on a roll; a Philadelphia "specialty."

clapper—the "tongue" of a bell.

constitution—the basic laws or principles that are used to govern a state, nation, or other organization.

convene—to gather together for a meeting.

delegate—a person who has been appointed to represent another person or group.

executive—the branch of government that manages and directs the affairs of a city, state, or nation.

freshwater port—A port located on a river or lake, as opposed to an ocean.

incorporated—legally established.

judicial—the branch of government that runs the courts and interprets the law.

jury—an appointed group of people who decide if someone is innocent or guilty of breaking the law.

legislative—the branch of government that makes the laws.

Mason-Dixon Line—the boundary between Pennsylvania and Maryland that divides the North from the South.

metropolitan area—a large city and its suburbs.

pagoda—a type of tower with a roof that curves upward, found in China, Japan, or other Eastern countries.

ratification—formal approval of something.

renovation—improvement of a house or other structure by cleaning, repairing, or rebuilding it.

restoration—bringing something back to a former, better state. Similar to renovation.

row houses—a series of houses connected by their side walls.

sculling—a type of boating that uses a light shell and a special type of oar.

union—a formal organization of workers trying to improve their working conditions.